English

Age 7-8

Contents

C000259518

Activities

Quick Tests

Alison Head and Louis Fidge

Word families

Many **words belong** to word families. Being able to spell one word in the family can help you to spell the rest.

spoon

moon

balloon

1 Put these words in their correct families. The first one has been done for you.

a light	d goat	g fright	j bright
b boat	e play	h tame	k hay
c name	f frame	i loan	l lay

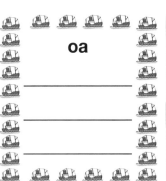

ight

light

_____

_____

oa

_____

_____

_____

ame

_____

_____

_____

ay

_____

_____

_____

2 Write two more words for each of these word families.

a	stain	lain	_____ _____
b	allow	bow	_____ _____
c	plate	grate	_____ _____
d	sail	pail	_____ _____
e	book	rook	_____ _____
f	tear	near	_____ _____
g	teach	preach	_____ _____
h	spent	lent	_____ _____
i	swell	fell	_____ _____
j	hive	strive	_____ _____

Spelling verbs

When we add *ing* to a verb, we have to **take care** with spelling.

Several verbs ending in *e* (like *smile*) lose the *e* when we add *ing*.

Several verbs with a short vowel sound in the middle, like the *u* in *run*, double the final consonant.

Kate is smil**ing**.

Rob is ru**nn**ing.

1 Look at each verb. Then circle its correct *ing* spelling.

a	hope	hopping	hopeing	hoping
b	bake	bakeing	baking	bakking
c	clap	claping	clapeing	clapping
d	spin	spining	spineing	spinning
e	win	wining	winning	wineing
f	lose	losing	lossing	loseing
g	shut	shuting	shuteing	shutting
h	fit	fitting	fiteing	fiting
i	make	makeing	making	makking
j	swim	swimmming	swimming	swiming
k	slip	slipping	slipeing	sliping

2 Write these verbs with their correct *ing* spelling.

a ride + ing = _____

b plan + ing = _____

c sit + ing = _____

d shop + ing = _____

e stare + ing = _____

f jog + ing = _____

g slip + ing = _____

h hate + ing = _____

i rub + ing = _____

j hit + ing = _____

k raise + ing = _____

l shake + ing = _____

Speaking and listening (1)

Being able to speak clearly and listen carefully to others is very important. Interviewing someone helps to practise these skills.

1 Interview a friend about their favourite hobby. Perhaps they are in a sports team, or have a pet. You will need to ask some questions to find out information. Make sure you listen carefully to their answers.

Plan some questions you can ask. You do not need to write in full sentences as these are notes to help you to give a good interview.

a _____

b _____

c _____

d _____

e _____

2 Can you remember what your friend said? Write an account of what you remember in the box.

Prefixes

You can add prefixes to the **beginning** of some words to change their meanings.

happy

unhappy

Different prefixes mean different things.

un = not   *dis* = not   *re* = again   *pre* = before

1 Choose *un* or *dis* to make these words mean the opposite. Then write the new words.

a __un__ + able   = __unable__   f _____ + popular = _____

b _____ + seen   = _____   g _____ + do   = _____

c _____ + qualify = _____   h _____ + appear = _____

d _____ + usual   = _____   i _____ + own   = _____

e _____ + obey   = _____   j _____ + tidy   = _____

2 Write the correct prefix *un*, *dis*, *re* or *pre.* Then list the completed words in the correct boxes.

a _____well   d _____pare   g _____agree   j _____lucky

b _____cycle   e _____turn   h _____honest   k _____build

c _____allow   f _____kind   i _____dict   l _____vious

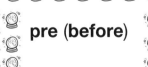
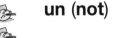

un (not)   **dis (not)**   **re (again)**   **pre (before)**

_____   _____   _____   _____

_____   _____   _____   _____

_____   _____   _____   _____

_____   _____   _____   _____

5

Synonyms

Synonyms are words that have **similar meanings**.

fast

speedy

quick

Choosing synonyms for words we use a lot can make our writing more interesting.

1 Write two synonyms from the box for each word.

> glum pleased huge tiny unhappy freezing small excellent
> after joyful brilliant large chilly unkind mean later

a big   _____ _____

b little   _____ _____

c good   _____ _____

d cold   _____ _____

e nasty   _____ _____

f then   _____ _____

g sad   _____ _____

h happy   _____ _____

2 Write a synonym for each of these words.

a run   _____

b laugh   _____

c wet   _____

d hungry   _____

e speak   _____

f seat   _____

g fast   _____

h old   _____

i walk   _____

j closed   _____

k begin   _____

l simple   _____

Speech marks

Speech marks, or 'inverted commas', show that someone is **speaking**. We write what the person says between the speech marks.

"Today is my birthday," said Jack.
Molly said, "Happy birthday."

1 Add speech marks at the end of the speech in these sentences. Take care to put them the right side of the comma. Use the examples above to help you.

a "My best friend is Max, said Joel.

b "I love football, said Rita.

c "We are going swimming today, said Mum.

d Martin said, "That is my bag.

e "I have a new puppy, said Alfie.

f The teacher said, "It is raining today.

g Dad shouted, "Do not forget your coat!

h "Let us watch TV, said Sophie.

2 Find the speech in these sentences and add the speech marks.

a I am going skating tomorrow, said Heather.

b Sarah said, That is not fair!

c Harry sighed, I love chocolate cake!

d I would like a drink please, said Lucy.

e Look at my new bike, said Katy.

f The bus driver called out, This is your stop!

g Time to tidy up, shouted Mrs Moors.

h Gran said, See you soon!

Verbs

Verbs tell us what a person or thing is **doing**.

A fish **swims**.

Choosing the right verb can also tell the reader exactly how a person or thing does something.

This frog **hops**.

This frog **leaps**.

1 Underline the verb in each sentence.

a The sun shines.

b Birds fly.

c Molly reads a book.

d Sam paints a picture.

e Chris watches television.

f Matthew waits for the train.

g Charlotte munches her lunch.

h The lorries turn a corner.

i He shuts the door.

j The school bell rings.

2 Write the verbs in the box next to the verb with similar meanings.

| dash | slumber | see | build | peer | sprint |
| watch | jog | snooze | create | doze | assemble |

run _____ _____ _____

make _____ _____ _____

sleep _____ _____ _____

look _____ _____ _____

More verbs

The **tense** of a verb tells us whether something is happening now or whether it has happened already.

I **am eating** the cake.

This is the **present tense**.

I **ate** the cake.

This is the **past tense**.

1 Underline the correct past tense verb to complete each sentence. The verbs are in **bold**.

a Rob **walks walked** home last night.

b Last year I **went goes** to France.

c My glass **is was** full before I drank my juice.

d Mum **fixed fixes** my bike this morning.

e Last Saturday we **bakes baked** a cake.

f Yesterday I **swaps swapped** a toy with Ben.

g Dad **drives drove** us to the party last Tuesday.

h Mum **hid hides** my presents before last Christmas.

i I **worry worried** before last week's test.

j Sally **tried tries** to catch the last bus yesterday.

Complete this chart by filling in the missing past and present verbs.

Present	Past		Present	Past
a give	_____		g _____	copied
b _____	tapped		h wash	_____
c _____	skipped		i speak	_____
d mix	_____		j _____	built
e bring	_____		k am	_____
f _____	caught		l _____	grew

9

Speaking and listening (2)

Giving oral (spoken) reports and presentations helps you to speak clearly and listen carefully.

1 You are going to give a presentation to a grown-up about your favourite book. Answer these questions to help you plan your presentation.

a What is the title of your favourite book? Who is the author?

_____

b Why is it your favourite? What do you love about the book?

_____

c Who is your favourite character, and why?

_____

d What, in your opinion, is the best thing that happens in the book?

_____

e How did the story end? Were the problems resolved?

_____

2 Plan an oral report on an event at school. It could be a play, sports day, fundraising event – you choose. Make notes to help you plan your report.

a What was the event?

_____

b Why was the event held?

_____

c Describe what happened at the event.

_____

d How did you feel about what happened?

_____

e Would you want to take part in a similar event if you got the chance? Give reasons for your answer.

_____

More about writing speech

When we write what someone says, we also need to write **who** is saying it.

"My hat is blue," **said Paul**.

We can say more about what the person is saying, like whether it is a question or a reply.

"Where did you get it?" **asked Alex**.

"From the junkyard," **replied Chris**.

1 Circle the name of the person speaking in each sentence. Then underline the word that tells us more about what they are saying. The first one is done for you.

a "Stop it!" <u>shouted</u> (Jack).

b "Where is my book?" asked Sophie.

c "It is on your bed," answered Mum.

d "Shall we go out?" suggested Tim.

e "Good idea!" replied Ella.

f Jake grumbled, "My head hurts."

g Lucy asked, "What time is it?"

h Dad explained, "The toy is broken."

i Sally demanded, "Why can't I?"

j Mum replied, "Because it is late."

2 Underline the best word in bold to complete each sentence.

a "I am going out," **said asked** James.

b "Where are you going?" **explained asked** Chloe.

c "I need to post a letter," **demanded replied** James.

d "Could you post one for me?" **asked argued** Ryan.

e "Of course," **asked answered** James.

f "It is to my friend Asher," **requested explained** Ryan.

g "It is raining," **commented queried** Chloe.

h "No it's not," **questioned argued** James.

i "It is!" **giggled shouted** Chloe angrily.

j "I am going anyway," **insisted asked** James.

An or a?

The sound of a word's first letter shows you whether to say *a* or *an*. If the word starts with a vowel sound, use *an*. If it starts with a consonant sound, use *a*.

Be careful – it's about the way things **sound**. So you say 'an hour' not 'a hour'. *H* is a consonant, but in the word *hour* it makes a vowel sound. Say it out loud to check.

an apple

a banana

1 *An* or *a*? Underline the correct word in bold in each sentence.

a I can see **a an** herd of elephants.

b I'd like **a an** orange.

c Would you like **a an** drink?

d There's **a an** insect in my hair!

e Would you like **a an** cup of tea?

f I'm putting together **a an** album of photos for my nana.

g I'm making **a an** cheese sandwich.

h I'm getting **a an** cat next week.

2 Underline the correct word in bold in these trickier sentences.

a I need **a an** x-ray because I hurt my leg.

b I'm moving to **a an** house in the country this summer.

c I'll be ready in **a an** hour.

d **A An** UFO is an unidentified flying object.

e That has **a an** unknown answer.

f It is **a an** honour to be here.

g I'd like to be **a an** extra in a film.

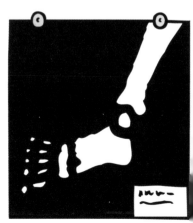

Suffixes *er* and *est*

We can make adjectives **tell us more** about the person or thing they are describing by adding letters such as *er* or *est*.

These groups of letters are called suffixes.

a big present   a bigg**er** present   the bigg**est** present

1 Fill in the gaps. Look carefully at how the spelling changes when you add *er* or *est*.

		Add *er*	**Add** *est*
a	quick	_____	quickest
b	long	longer	_____
c	nice	_____	nicest
d	_____	later	latest
e	hot	hotter	_____
f	fat	_____	fattest
g	_____	angrier	angriest

2 Underline the *er* or *est* word in each sentence that is spelt wrong, then write it again correctly.

a My jokes are much funnyer than Ben's, but Andy's are the funniest of all.

_____

b Ginny lives closer to the park than we do, but Sally lives the closeest of all.

_____

c I need a bigger pair of shoes, but even the bigest in the shop do not fit me.

_____

d Yesterday was sunier than Monday, but tomorrow is supposed to be the sunniest day so far this year.

_____

e I changed my picture to make the girl in it look happyer, but the boy has the happiest face.

_____

13

Writing non-fiction: paragraphs

Paragraphs (collections of sentences) can help make your writing interesting and **easier to understand**. They break writing up into sections.

In letters, paragraphs are used to introduce new ideas and points of view.

1 Put a mark to show where a new paragraph could start in this letter. One has been done for you. Use this example to help you.

I'm really enjoying my guitar lessons! My tutor is lovely, and he is teaching me lots of great songs. He has given me lots of chances to perform live, too. ‖Firstly, I have a chance to take part in a summer concert at the Sage, Gateshead – so exciting! Secondly, he has arranged for me to join in with a group who play for dances at The Irish Club in Newcastle. Finally, he asked if I could play with a group at an outdoor festival in Exhibition Park – and they said yes! As a result, I am practising every night, because I have so many new songs to learn. I'm quite busy.

2 Write a letter about something you have done recently. Use these connectives to help you organise your ideas into paragraphs.

a Firstly,

_____

b Secondly,

_____

c On the other hand,

_____

d Finally,

_____

e As a result,

_____

Words ending in *sure* and *ture*

Sure and *ture* are similar spelling patterns. Listen carefully when you say the words out loud and you will **hear** the difference.

treasure

picture

1 These words all end in *sure*. Learn how to spell them using the LOOK, COVER, WRITE, CHECK method. Then write a sentence for each to show their meaning.

a sure _____

b pressure _____

c unsure _____

d measure _____

e pleasure _____

f treasure _____

g leisure _____

2 Now learn these spellings using the LOOK, COVER, WRITE, CHECK method. Then write a sentence for each to show their meaning.

a capture _____

b future _____

c creature _____

d culture _____

e lecture _____

f picture _____

g nature _____

Spellings that use *y* when they have an *i* sound

Sometimes *y* in a word makes an *i* sound. Read the word out loud and you can hear the *i* sound.

pyramid

1 Learn these spellings using the LOOK, COVER, WRITE, CHECK method.

a myth _____

b Egypt _____

c gym _____

d pyramid _____

e mystery _____

f hymn _____

g rhythm _____

h mysterious _____

i gymnastics _____

j mythical _____

Ask a grown-up to test you to see if you can remember the spellings.

2 Write a sentence for each of the words to show that you understand the meaning.

a mythical _____

b mystery _____

c hymn _____

d gym _____

e rhythm _____

f pyramid _____

Spelling *ou*

Sometimes, the *ou* blend of letters makes the short sound *u*. Say these words out loud to **hear the difference**.

mouth ➡ **ow** sound   **you**ngster ➡ **u** sound

1 Learn these spellings using the LOOK, COVER, WRITE, CHECK method.

a young _____   g rough _____

b touch _____   h cousin _____

c double _____   i encourage _____

d trouble _____   j tough _____

e country _____   k enough _____

f youngster _____

Ask a grown-up to test you to see if you can remember the spellings.

2 Write a sentence for each of the words to show that you understand the meaning.

a double _____

b country _____

c encourage _____

d enough _____

e rough _____

f touch _____

Adding the suffix *ly* to an adjective to make an adverb

Many adjectives can be changed into adverbs by adding the suffix *ly*.

sad ➡ sad**ly**

1 Change these adjectives to adverbs by adding the suffix *ly*.

a glad ➡ _____

b sudden ➡ _____

c slow ➡ _____

d quick ➡ _____

e beautiful ➡ _____

f soft ➡ _____

g loud ➡ _____

h sharp ➡ _____

i quiet ➡ _____

2 Change these adverbs back to adjectives.

a thankfully ➡ _____

b perfectly ➡ _____

c slowly ➡ _____

d suddenly ➡ _____

e angrily ➡ _____

f beautifully ➡ _____

g gracefully ➡ _____

h quickly ➡ _____

i certainly ➡ _____

Alphabetical order

If a list of words all start with the same letter, we can use the next letter to put them in alphabetical order. This is useful when you are looking things up in a dictionary.

ball

bed

a comes before *e* in the alphabet, so *ball* comes before *bed*.

1 Write these names in alphabetical order.

Arthur	Ashley
Abigail	Amy
Anthony	Aiden
Alice	Attia

1 _____   5 _____

2 _____   6 _____

3 _____   7 _____

4 _____   8 _____

2 Look at the first two letters of each animal to help you find them in the alphabetical index. Then write down the page number.

a bats _____

b birds _____

c chickens _____

d ducks _____

e cows _____

f bees _____

g cats _____

h deer _____

i crows _____

j dogs _____

Animals	Page Number
bats	55
bees	12
birds	18
cats	50
chickens	33
cows	29
crows	82
deer	46
dogs	6
ducks	63

The suffix *cian*

The suffix *cian* makes the sound 'shun'. Say the word **out loud** to hear the sound.

magi**cian**

1 Learn these spellings using the LOOK, COVER, WRITE, CHECK method.

a musician _____

b electrician _____

c magician _____

d politician _____

e mathematician _____

f physician _____

g optician _____

h technician _____

Ask a grown-up to test you to see if you can remember your spellings.

2 Now write a sentence to show what each person does as a job.

a musician _____

b electrician _____

c magician _____

d politician _____

e mathematician _____

f physician _____

g optician _____

h technician _____

20

Pronouns

Pronouns can sometimes be used instead of nouns.

Tom likes **dogs**.   dogs = noun

Tom likes **them**.   them = pronoun

When you are talking about yourself, you use *I*, *me* or *my*. These are all pronouns.

I like **my** dinner.

Aaron plays with **me**.

1 Underline the pronouns in these sentences. Look carefully as some sentences contain more than one!

a I ate my lunch.

b Will you be at school?

c I went to his party.

d Ali walked with them.

e We are going fishing.

f Ruby is my best friend.

g This game is mine.

h I played with her.

i Pete walks his dog.

j The boys did their homework.

2 Rewrite these sentences, replacing the bold nouns with a pronoun from the brackets.

a Emma opened **Emma's** presents. (his her their)

_____

b **The boys** gobbled their sandwiches. (We They You)

_____

c **Lucy** is my cousin. (He She It)

_____

d **My teacher and I** tidied the classroom. (We I They)

_____

e The king sat on **the king's** throne. (my their his)

_____

f **Mum and Dad** are going out tonight. (We They You)

_____

Collective nouns

Collective nouns describe **groups of things**.

A **herd** of elephants

A **pack** of wolves

These are collective nouns.

1 Pick a word from the box to complete these collective nouns.

a a flock of _____

b a swarm of _____

c a flight of _____

d a deck of _____

e a bunch of _____

f a litter of _____

g a pride of _____

h a gaggle of _____

i a troupe of _____

j a shoal of _____

cards
fish
sheep
monkeys
geese
stairs
bees
lions
puppies
flowers

2 Draw lines to match each thing on the left with their collective noun on the right.

a horses   pod

b birds   herd

c cars   group

d books   fleet

e musicians   library

f dolphins   flock

Commas

Commas tell readers when to **pause**.

Paul had tea, then he went home.

They also separate items in a **list**.

We bought apples, bananas, grapes and pears.

1 Look carefully at the commas in these sentences. Circle the commas in lists. Underline the commas which show a pause.

a Joe, my brother, is eight years old.

b For lunch, we had sausages, chips, peas and carrots.

c I'm wearing trousers, a shirt, socks and shoes.

d Actually, it is quite warm today.

e The bag split, so the shopping went everywhere.

f In stories, the knight always kills the dragon.

g You need sugar, flour, eggs and butter to bake a cake.

h Anyway, it was all fine in the end.

2 Add commas to these sentences. Read the words out loud to help you decide where the pauses or lists are.

a Mrs Smith my teacher marked my work.

b My best friends are Chris Sam and Jo.

c In the end I chose the blue coat.

d Although it was late we played one more game.

e Last night after Dad came home we watched TV.

f Alex my best friend lives next door.

g At the zoo we saw elephants lions camels and giraffes.

h Eventually I found the missing book.

Homophones

Homophones are words that **sound the same** but have a **different meaning**. Sometimes they are also spelt the same way but have different meanings. Others are spelt differently but sound the same.

ball

bawl

1 Choose the correct word to complete each sentence. Cross out the WRONG word.

a I am happy to **accept except** this award.

b What is the **affect effect** if I add salt to this ice?

c Catch this **ball bawl**!

d Pop a **berry bury** on top of each cake.

e Don't **brake break** that vase!

f I am going to the **fair fare** tonight.

g That's **grate great**!

2 Write a sentence for each word to show you understand what it means.

a groan _____

b grown _____

c here _____

d hear _____

e heel _____

f heal _____

g knot _____

h not _____

Writing instructions

Written instructions tell us **how to do** something.

To get to my house, turn right at the school gates. Then, turn left at the roundabout. I live at number 32.

Good instructions give us the important information in the right order.

1 Put these instructions for making a banana smoothie in the right order by numbering them 1–6.

a _____ Serve immediately.

b _____ Place banana in a blender with milk.

c _____ Pour into a chilled glass.

d _____ Ask an adult to blend the ingredients until smooth.

e _____ Peel one banana.

f _____ Add one scoop of vanilla ice cream.

2 Write these instructions in the right order.

Use your finger or a pencil to make a hole about 3 cm deep. Cover with soil. Keep soil just damp until seedling appears. Fill the pot with soil, leaving a gap at the top. Drop a sunflower seed into the hole. Find a small flower pot.

a _____

b _____

c _____

d _____

e _____

f _____

The suffix *ation*

The suffix *ation* can be added to verbs to make nouns – clever!

inform ➡ inform**ation**

If the word you are adding *ation* to ends in e, drop the e before you add the suffix.

adore ➡ ador**ation**

1 Add the suffix *ation* to these words to make new words.

a inform ➡ _____

b adore ➡ _____

c prepare ➡ _____

d admire ➡ _____

e condense ➡ _____

f stagnate ➡ _____

2 Write a sentence to show what each word means. If you need help, use a dictionary.

a vegetation _____

b frustration _____

c agitation _____

d fascination _____

e dedication _____

f decoration _____

Spelling *ei, eigh, ey*

ei, eigh and *ey* can all **sound the same** in words, even though they use different letter strings.

sov**ei**n

eight

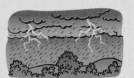
gr**ey**

1 Draw a line to match the words to their correct letter pattern.

a eight

b vein

c freight

d rein

e they

ei

eigh

ey

f obey

g sovereign

h weight

i prey

j grey

2 Underline the *ei, eigh* and *ey* words in these sentences.

a I weighed out a kilogram of apples.

b My dog obeys all my commands.

c I did a survey about which biscuits people like best.

d Father Christmas rides on a sleigh.

e That horse neighed at me!

f My neighbour is called Susan.

g They love swimming in the sea.

h Spiders have eight hairy legs.

i I can see rich veins of chocolate running through this ice cream – delicious!

The suffix *sion*

The suffix *sion* makes the sound 'shun'.
Say the word **out loud** to hear the sound.

television

1 Join each word to the correct description with a line.

a comprehension   Dividing something into smaller pieces

b division   Something to watch programmes on

c television   Being able to see

d discussion   Talking about something

e confusion   Finding something difficult to understand

f admission   Understanding something

g expression   Entrance fee; admitting something

h vision   A look on someone's face

2 Complete the words by adding *sion*. Then choose six of the words and write sentences to show you understand the meaning.

a inva_____   f expres_____

b pen_____   g ten_____

c mis_____   h occa_____

d ses_____   i pas_____

e ver_____   j permis_____

_____

_____

_____

_____

_____

_____

Singular and plural

When we change from singular to plural, sometimes the spellings change and sometimes the whole word changes. Sometimes the word stays exactly the same.

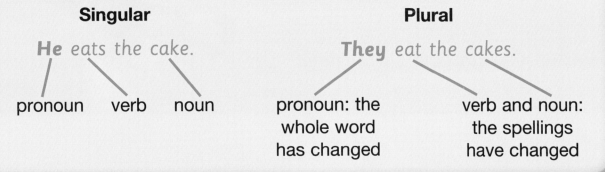

Singular	Plural
He eats the cake.	**They** eat the cakes.
pronoun verb noun	pronoun: the whole word has changed verb and noun: the spellings have changed

1 Fill in all the plurals. The first one has been done for you.

	Singular	Plural			Singular	Plural
a	he runs	_they run_		f	I walk	_____
b	she swims	_____		g	I eat	_____
c	I laugh	_____		h	she pushes	_____
d	he sleeps	_____		i	he wishes	_____
e	she builds	_____		j	I hope	_____

2 Write these sentences in the plural, making sure the nouns, verbs and pronouns are all plural.

a She picks the flower.

_____

b He kicks the ball.

_____

c I sharpen the pencil.

_____

d She washes the car.

_____

Conjunctions

Conjunctions are words that can **join** two short sentences together.

I took my umbrella.
It was raining.

I took my umbrella,
because it was raining.

1 Underline the conjunctions in these sentences.

a I turned the TV on when my favourite programme started.

b I did my homework, so I could go and play.

c I called for Asif, but he was out.

d Kelly likes bananas, but I like apples.

e I went to bed, because I was tired.

f I stayed at home, while Mum went shopping.

g Drew was just leaving when we arrived.

h I could wear my jeans or I could wear a skirt.

2 Choose a conjunction from the box to make the two short sentences into one sentence. Write each new sentence.

a I got a drink. I was thirsty.

_____

b Chris wants a skateboard. Mum said no.

_____

c Luke was three. I was born.

_____

d We waited. Dad packed up the car.

_____

e I could go bowling. I could go swimming.

_____

| but |
| when |
| or |
| because |
| while |

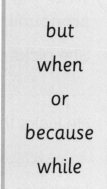

First and third person accounts

If I write about what I am doing, this is called a **first person** account.

I kicked the ball.

If **I** write about what someone else does,
this is called a **third person** account.

Ella kicked the ball.

1 Read these sentences, then decide whether each one is a first person or third person account. Tick the correct box.

	First person	Third person
a Sean lost his bag.	☐	☐
b I had chicken pox.	☐	☐
c My cat is called Monty.	☐	☐
d They went to America on holiday.	☐	☐
e Dad missed the train.	☐	☐
f I live in a town.	☐	☐
g Lee and Kerry played football.	☐	☐
h I walk to school.	☐	☐

2 Read this third person account of life in the Handy family. Imagine you are Sarah Handy and rewrite it as a first person account.

The Handy family live in a small house in Bridge Street. They have a dog and a cat. Sarah Handy plays netball and is learning to play the violin. Her best friend is called Leah.

_____

_____

_____

_____

_____

Test 1 **Prefixes**

A **prefix** is a group of letters we put **in front** of a word.

Prefixes **change the meaning** of the word.

well

unwell

Choose the prefix *un* or *dis* to complete each word.

1. _____pack

2. _____well

3. _____place

4. _____trust

5. _____fair

6. _____happy

7. _____agree

8. _____may

9. _____load

10. _____bolt

11. _____honest

12. _____do

13. _____arm

14. _____charge

15. _____please

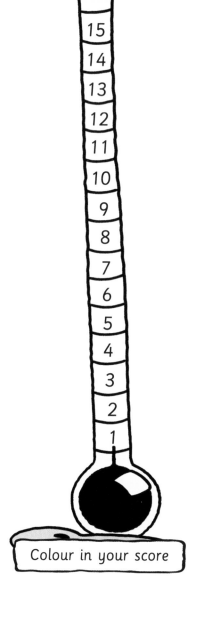

15
14
13
12
11
10
9
8
7
6
5
4
3
2
1

Colour in your score

Test 2 Verbs

A **verb** tells us what someone **is doing** or what **is happening**.

*Anna **is riding** her bike.*

Choose the best verb to complete each sentence.

1. The rabbit _____ into the burrow. (disappeared/spoke)

2. The child _____ in a whisper. (spoke/chased)

3. The bull _____ the boy across the field. (drew/chased)

4. I _____ up all the mess. (brushed/groaned)

5. Abdi _____ a lovely picture. (painted/crashed)

6. Who is _____ at the door? (eating/knocking)

7. The girls were _____ lemonade. (drinking/painting)

8. The injured man _____ with pain. (turned/groaned)

9. The lady was _____ a pram. (raining/pushing)

10. The sun is _____ in the sky. (shining/shouting)

11. A lion _____ loudly. (smiled/roared)

12. The car _____ into the wall. (crashed/crushed)

13. The dragon _____ its wings. (flagged/flapped)

14. The frog _____ onto the log. (hoped/hopped)

15. A letter _____ through the letter box. (came/screamed)

15
14
13
12
11
10
9
8
7
6
5
4
3
2
1

Colour in your score

33

Test 3 Phonemes

A **phoneme** is the **smallest unit of sound**. A phoneme may be made up
of **one or more letters** which make **one sound**.

b + oa + t = boat

This word is made by using **three phonemes**.

Choose the correct phoneme to complete each word.

1. m_____n (oo/ir)

2. tr_____t (ee/ea)

3. gr_____ (ow/oo)

4. gl_____ (ue/oo)

5. r_____d (oa/ow)

6. cl_____ (aw/ow)

7. p_____nt (au/ai)

8. b_____n (ir/ur)

9. _____l (ay/ow)

10. th_____sty (oo/ir)

11. yesterd_____ (ai/ay)

12. narr_____ (ow/aw)

13. r_____nd (ow/ou)

14. s_____cer (ou/au)

15. b_____l (oi/oa)

Colour in your score

Test 4 Comprehension (1)

Comprehension exercises check that you understand the things you have read.

Read the text and answer the questions.

The dragon stretched out her purple wings, and yawned. A puff of smoke burst out of her nostrils, and a flame licked out of her mouth. She flexed one strong, scaly leg, then another. Her black claws clacked on the stone.

She stood up, and looked happily at her nest. Three green eggs lay there, rocking backwards and forwards. A chirping noise got louder and then there was a loud crack. One of the eggs split open, and a tiny head popped out. The other eggs opened and soon three little dragons were nestling down in their bed. The mother dragon stroked them with her paws, and sang them to sleep.

1. What colour were the dragon's wings? _____

2. What came out of the dragon's nostrils? _____

3. What came out of the dragon's mouth? _____

4. What were the dragon's legs like? _____

5. What colour were her claws? _____

6. What was in the nest? _____

7. What noise did the baby dragons make? _____

8. How many babies were there? _____

9. Once all the babies hatched, what did the mother

    dragon do? _____

10. How do you think the mother dragon felt?

    _____

Colour in your score

Test 5 Punctuation marks

Punctuation marks make writing **easier to read**.

Most sentences end with a **full stop**.

This is an alien.

If it is a **question**, a **question mark** is needed.

What is this?

We put an **exclamation mark** when we **feel strongly** about something.

What a strange alien!

Put in the missing punctuation mark in each sentence.

1. Where do you come from

2. What a funny name

3. The spaceship landed

4. A door opened slowly

5. Run for your life

6. Who is there

7. What do you want

8. It's not fair

9. This is terrible

10. The sun set in the sky

11. The bees buzzed near the flowers

12. How did the car crash

13. When did the letter come

14. Stop that at once

15. We have sausages and chips for tea

Colour in your score

Test 6 Speech marks

When we write down what people say we use **speech marks**.

The **words the person says** go **inside** the speech marks.

The lumberjack said, "I cut down trees."

Fill in the missing speech marks.

1. Little Bo Peep said, I've lost my sheep.

2. The mouse said, I ran up the clock.

3. Humpty Dumpty said, I fell off the wall.

4. Incy Wincy Spider said, I climbed up the water spout.

5. Little Jack Horner said, I sat in the corner.

6. I marched up the hill, said the grand old Duke of York.

7. I went to London, said Dick Whittington.

8. I met a wolf, said Little Red Riding Hood.

9. I climbed a beanstalk, said Jack.

10. I ran away, said the gingerbread man.

11. Hansel said, I got lost in a wood.

12. I went to the ball, Cinderella said.

13. Old King Cole said, I'm a merry old soul.

14. I made some tarts, said the Queen of Hearts.

15. I'm very ugly, the troll said.

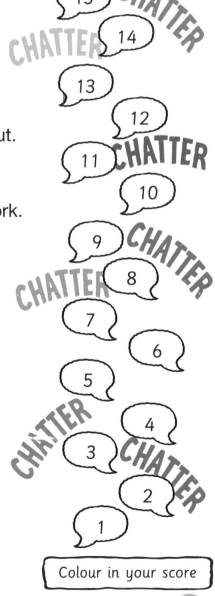

Colour in your score

Test 7 Alphabetical order

Many books are arranged in **alphabetical order**.

anteater **b**ear **c**amel

These words are arranged in alphabetical order according to their **first** letter.

d**ee**r d**o**g d**u**ck

These words are arranged in alphabetical order according to their **second** letter.

Order these words according to their first letter.

1. bat dog cat _____

2. goat elephant fox _____

3. hen kangaroo jaguar _____

4. ostrich monkey lion _____

5. rat seal penguin _____

6. zebra swan panda _____

7. hamster mouse donkey beetle _____

8. ox worm donkey giraffe _____

Order these words according to their second letter.

9. crab cow cat _____

10. bird bull bear _____

11. parrot pike pelican _____

12. shark sardine snake _____

13. trout tiger turtle toad _____

14. giraffe gnu goat gerbil _____

15. bee badger bird buffalo _____

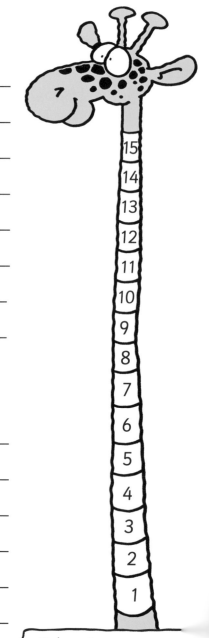

15
14
13
12
11
10
9
8
7
6
5
4
3
2
1

Colour in your score

Test 8 Verbs: past tense

This is happening **now**, so the verb is in the **present tense**.

This happened in the **past**, so the verb is in the **past tense**.

Join up each verb with its past tense.

1.	walk	hopped
2.	hop	moved
3.	carry	copied
4.	move	walked
5.	arrive	held
6.	beg	carried
7.	copy	spoke
8.	hold	wrote
9.	bring	came
10.	see	taught
11.	speak	arrived
12.	take	brought
13.	teach	took
14.	write	begged
15.	come	saw

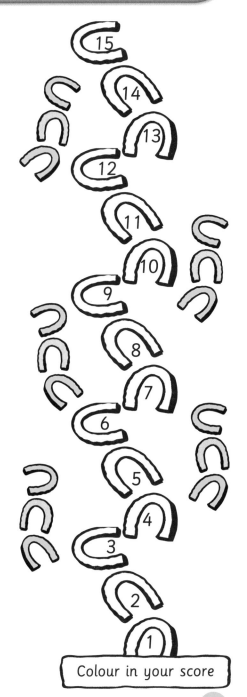

Colour in your score

Test 9 Comprehension (2) – dialogue

It is important that you understand what is meant by words written in the dialogue that you read.

Read the dialogue and answer the questions.

> "What do you want to be when you grow up?"
>
> "I'm not sure, Mum. Maybe a doctor ... or an astronaut ... or a vet."
>
> "That sounds exciting! I used to want to be a teacher when I was a girl. I wanted to be a mummy, too."
>
> "Well, you are a mummy. But I didn't know you ever wanted to be a teacher. Why didn't you do that?"
>
> "When I was at university, I started volunteering at a centre for homeless people. I saw that lots of people needed help, and I really enjoyed what I was doing. When I left university, I got a job working with the charity Shelter – and stayed there. I love my job!"
>
> "That's brilliant. I hope I am as happy in the job I choose. In the meantime, I'd better work hard at school."

1. Who is talking?

   _____

2. What does the child say they might like to do as a job?

   _____

3. Why did the mother not become a teacher?

   _____

   _____

4. Does the mother enjoy her job?

   _____

5. What does the daughter say she needs to do at school?

   _____

5

4

3

2

1

Colour in your score

Test 10 **Comprehension (3) – instructions**

Instructions tell you how to do things. It is important
that you understand what you read.

Read the instructions for making a monster mask and answer the questions.

What to do:	What you need:
1. Draw your monster design on the card.	Card
2. Cut the shape out.	Masking tape
3. With a grown-up, cut out eye and mouth holes.	Paints
	Scissors
4. Paint the mask and leave it to dry.	Glitter glue
5. Add details with markers and glitter glue.	Thick markers
6. Tape a piece of elastic to the back of the mask so you can wear it!	Elastic

1. What materials do you need for making the mask?

    _____

    _____

2. What do you do first?

    _____

3. What can a grown-up help you to do?

    _____

4. What do you need to do after you paint your mask?

    _____

5. What do you use to add details to your mask?

    _____

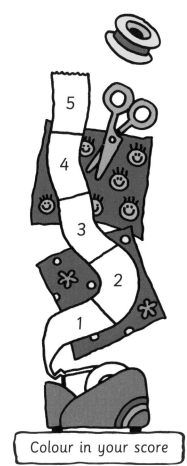

Colour in your score

Open-ended questions do not
have one 'right' or 'wrong' answer.
You need to **infer** the answer.

Read the text and answer the questions.

The girl looked up at the sky. The moonlight fell like a silver veil, touching the garden and lighting everything with a silver glow. She listened carefully, her head on one side. Was that an owl, or something magical?

Suddenly, the bushes started to rustle. A snuffling noise began, and the girl stepped backwards. She moved nearer to the door, and called her dog closer. Whatever was in there? Her breath came faster and made white clouds in the cold air. The dog started to growl, and showed her teeth.

First a small pointed nose and then a prickly head poked out of the undergrowth. "It's a hedgehog!" the girl laughed. She stroked the dog and put her inside, before coming back to watch a hedgehog and her babies bumble around the garden, rummaging among stones and leaves.

1. How do you think the girl felt when she was listening to the owl?

   _____

2. How do you think the girl felt when the bushes started to move?

   _____

3. Why do you think the girl's breathing got faster?

   _____

4. Why do you think the dog was growling?

   _____

5. What do you think the hedgehogs were looking for?

   _____

⑤
④
③
②
①

Colour in your score

Test 12 **Singular and plural**

A noun may be **singular** (when there is **only one** thing).

A noun may be **plural** (when there is **more** than one thing).

one bus (singular)   two buses (plural)

Complete these phrases.
Be careful with some of the spellings!

1. one chair, lots of _____

2. one fox, lots of _____

3. one coach, lots of _____

4. one bush, lots of _____

5. one glass, lots of _____

6. one berry, lots of _____

7. one child, lots of _____

8. one man, lots of _____

9. one _____, lots of bikes

10. one _____, lots of boxes

11. one _____, lots of bunches

12. one _____, lots of dishes

13. one _____, lots of copies

14. one _____, lots of lorries

15. one _____, lots of sheep

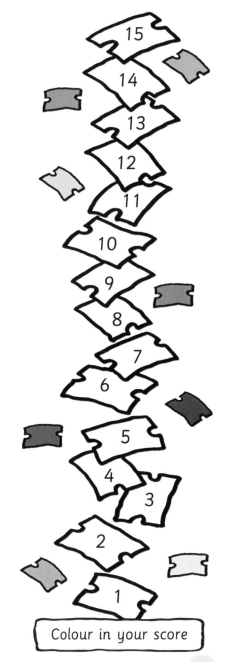

Colour in your score

Test 13 Handwriting (1)

Neat handwriting helps people to be able to read your work easily.

Write out these sentences in your best joined-up handwriting. Pay special attention to the shapes of the letters, and the way they are spaced out.

1. Today is my eighth birthday.

    _____

2. I got a bicycle from Mum and Dad.

    _____

3. Grandpa bought me a swing for the garden.

    _____

4. Mum made me a dinosaur cake.

    _____

5. There is also some amazing ice cream.

    _____

6. I can't wait to blow out the candles!

    _____

7. My friends are coming on Saturday for a party.

    _____

8. Dad has organised a treasure hunt.

    _____

9. He has bought real fossils as prizes.

    _____

10. He is going to bury them in the sandpit!

    _____

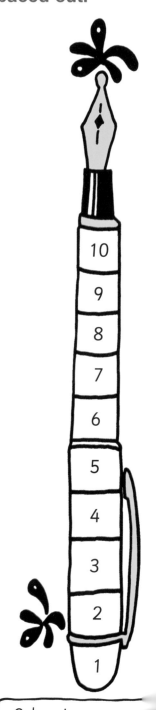

10
9
8
7
6
5
4
3
2
1

Colour in your scor

Test 14 Handwriting (2)

When your handwriting is neat it makes people want to read what you have written!

Write out these sentences in your best joined-up handwriting. Pay special attention to the shapes of the letters, and the way they are spaced out.

1. I like gardening with Nana.

    _____

2. She has given me a bed of my own.

    _____

3. I have planted some yellow pumpkin seeds.

    _____

4. I painted a Halloween pumpkin on a label.

    _____

5. Instead of buying a pumpkin, I am growing my own!

    _____

6. I have planted some gourds too.

    _____

7. Gourds have bumpy, stripy skin.

    _____

8. I can't wait to make a Halloween display!

    _____

9. Nana will show me how to make pumpkin pie.

    _____

10. I bet it tastes wonderful!

    _____

Colour in your score

Test 15 Dictation

Dictation is a really useful skill. It means listening when someone speaks, and writing down what they say. It is very useful for students taking notes, and many people use it as part of their jobs.

Ask a grown-up to read these sentences out loud, and write them down on a piece of paper.

1. My hamster is called Fred.

2. He is ginger and white.

3. He likes to eat sunflower seeds.

4. Fred has a wheel to play in.

5. He has a little house in his cage.

6. I fill it with soft bedding.

7. He needs fresh water every day.

8. I like holding Fred and letting him run up my arm.

9. He likes to play by running through big kitchen roll tubes.

10. I love my hamster very much.

How did you do?

Colour in your score

Test 16 Story writing (1) – settings

Settings – the places where your story happens – are important as they set the scene for the action.

Write a story about an adventure. Where – and when – does the action take place? Is it in the past or the future?

1. When is your story set?

   _____

2. Are there any cities? What do they look like?

   _____

3. What does the countryside look like?

   _____

4. What is the vegetation like?

   _____

5. Are there any animals?

   _____

6. What is the weather like?

   _____

7. What transport is there?

   _____

8. What do buildings look like?

   _____

9. What technology can you see?

   _____

10. What do the streets look like in the towns?

   _____

Colour in your score

Test 17 Subject and verb agreement

The **subject** (the main person or thing) and the **verb** in each sentence must **agree**.

The birds is flying. ☒

The birds are flying. ☑

Choose the correct form of the verb for each sentence.

1. Bells _____. (ring/rings)

2. The wind _____. (blow/blows)

3. A door _____. (open/opens)

4. Aeroplanes _____. (fly/flies)

5. An owl _____. (hoot/hoots)

6. Chickens _____ eggs. (lay/lays)

7. A rabbit _____ in a burrow. (live/lives)

8. Wolves _____. (howl/howls)

9. Mice _____. (squeak/squeaks)

10. I _____ my dinner. (eat/eats)

11. The children _____ to school. (go/goes)

12. Ben _____ a cold. (have/has)

13. The lady _____ some bread. (buy/buys)

14. Frogs _____. (hop/hops)

15. A cow _____ us milk. (give/gives)

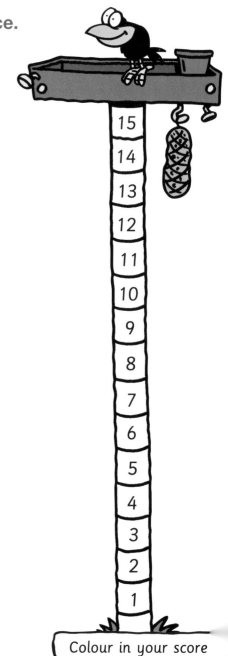

Colour in your score

Test 18 Collective nouns

A **collective noun** is the name given to a **group** of things.

*a **herd** of cows*

bunch   pile   library   flock   swarm
chest   shoal   fleet

Choose the best collective noun to complete each phrase.

1. a _____ of matches
2. a _____ of sheep
3. a _____ of bees
4. a _____ of drawers

5. a _____ of ships
6. a _____ of fish
7. a _____ of flowers
8. a _____ of books

sticks   stones   singers   athletes
soldiers   trees   bananas

Choose the best word to complete each phrase.

9. a choir of _____
10. an army of _____
11. a team of _____
12. a forest of _____

13. a bunch of _____
14. a bundle of _____
15. a pile of _____

Colour in your score

Test 19 Story writing (2) – characters

Characters are very important in any story.
If people don't care about the characters
in a story, they won't really care what
happens!

Use these questions to create a strong protagonist – the main character
in your story – for the story setting you planned on page 47.

1. What does your character look like? (tall/short)

   _____

2. How does your character dress? Describe their style of clothing.

   _____

3. What is their hair like? Do they have a special style or colour?

   _____

4. What does your character's face tell you about how they might act?

   _____

5. Does your character have an unusual voice?

   _____

6. How does your character act? Do they have any special skills or
   talents?

   _____

7. Does your character have a job, or are they studying?

   _____

8. Does your character have any transport?

   _____

9. Does your character have any brothers or sisters?

   _____

10. Does your character have any hobbies?

   _____

Colour in your scor

Test 20 Story writing (3) – planning

Planning a story is great fun – you get to decide what happens! Making a few notes about plot before you start writing your story can help to keep your story on track and moving forward.

Make notes in the boxes to plot and plan the story you created settings and characters for on pages 47 and 50.

1. Story opening – *make it exciting to make the reader want to read on*.

2. Build up – *what is the problem or challenge that needs to be overcome in your story*?

3. Main events – *what happens in your story*?

4. Who will overcome the problem, and how?

5. Conclusion – *how does your story end? Are all the problems solved*?

5

4

3

2

1

Colour in your score

Test 21 More prefixes

A **prefix** is a **group of letters** we put in front of a word.
Prefixes **change the meaning** of the word.

behave   **mis**behave

Choose the prefix *re* or *pre* to begin each word.

1. _____turn

5. _____caution

2. _____heat

6. _____mind

3. _____fix

7. _____fill

4. _____pare

8. _____fund

Choose the prefix *mis* or *ex* to begin each word.

9. _____judge

13. _____lead

10. _____handle

14. _____plode

11. _____port

15. _____pand

12. _____spell

Colour in your score

52

Test 22 Pronouns

A **pronoun** is a word that takes the place of a **noun**.

Ben cried when Ben hurt his leg.   Ben cried when **he** hurt his leg.

Choose the best pronoun to complete each sentence.

1. The lady went in the shop. _____ bought some apples. (He/She)

2. _____ am always busy. (We/I)

3. The boy shouted when _____ scored a goal. (he/it)

4. "Why are _____ late?" Mr Shah asked Abdi. (you/he)

5. "_____ are going to the park," the children said. (We/It)

6. _____ is a lovely day. (It/You)

7. Are _____ good at writing? (he/you)

8. _____ like playing games. (We/It)

9. The girl fell off her bike when _____ crashed. (she/you)

10. When the dog stopped _____ barked. (it/they)

11. The prince got up. _____ got dressed. (She/He)

12. I tried to lift the box but _____ was too heavy. (we/it)

13. When I shouted at the birds _____ flew away. (it/they)

14. The boy walked with the girl. _____ went into the park. (We/They)

15. When the man stopped _____ sat down. (you/he)

Colour in your score

Test 23 Using paragraphs in stories

Paragraphs help you to structure your story and interest your reader. When you are planning your story, it helps to plan some paragraphs.

Ideas for things to include in paragraphs will help you to write an exciting, well-structured story. Don't forget, you can also use new paragraphs to move between time and show flashbacks – and they are used in dialogue to show a new speaker.

Plan a story by writing notes for these paragraphs.

1. [   ] Introduction

2. [   ] Introduce main character

3. [   ] Introduce theme of the story

4. [   ] Introduce problem to be solved

5. [   ] Build-up of excitement

6. [   ] Develop other characters

7. [   ] Add suspense or change mood

8. [   ] Story climax

9. [   ] Resolution of problem

10. [   ] Strong final paragraph

STORY

10
9
8
7
6
5
4
3
2
1

Colour in your sco

Test 24 First and third person

When we are writing about **ourselves** we write in the **first person**. We use pronouns like *I* and *we*.

When we are writing about **others** we write in the **third person**. We use pronouns like *he, she, it* and *they*.

I called for Ben.
We went swimming.

Annie and Lucy were surprised when **they** opened the box.

Say if each of the pronouns marked in bold is in the first or third person.

1. **I** went to school.   _____

2. Tom went out when **he** finished washing up.   _____

3. The children chattered as **they** ate the bananas.   _____

4. When the dog appeared, **it** ran straight home.   _____

5. The flowers looked lovely. **They** were all different colours.   _____

6. **We** went to the cinema in the evening.   _____

7. May **I** have some, please?   _____

8. "**We** can do it!" Tom and Ben shouted.   _____

9. The machine made a loud noise when **it** was turned on.   _____

10. **I** am older than Sam.   _____

11. Mr Shah went to bed. **He** went straight to sleep.   _____

12. The lady was happy but **she** didn't smile.   _____

13. **They** ran for the bus.   _____

14. **I** was too frightened to move.   _____

15. **We** all like to win games.   _____

15
14
13
12
11
10
9
8
7
6
5
4
3
2
1
Push

Colour in your score

Test 25 Conjunctions

A **conjunction** is a **joining word**. It may be used to join **two sentences**.

I picked up the comic. I read it.   *I picked up the comic **and** read it.*

Choose the best conjunction to complete each sentence.

1. I had a bath _____ went to bed. (and/but)

2. An elephant is huge _____ an ant is small. (and/but)

3. I made a sandwich _____ ate it. (and/but)

4. Your towel is wet _____ mine is dry. (and/but)

5. A rabbit is fast _____ a snail is slow. (and/but)

6. I like swimming _____ playing rounders. (and/but)

7. You will get into trouble _____ you talk. (if/so)

8. I was wet _____ it was raining. (if/because)

9. It was hot _____ I took off my jumper. (so/because)

10. The door has been broken _____ I slammed it. (since/when)

11. I ran fast _____ I was late. (if/because)

12. We went for a walk _____ it was very hot. (so/although)

13. I will buy a lolly _____ you give me the money. (if/as)

14. You will get wet _____ you go in the rain. (if/so)

15. My uncle didn't come _____ I didn't see him. (so/if)

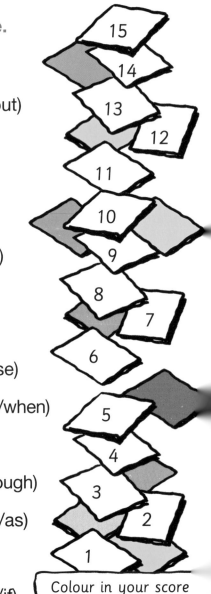

Colour in your score

56

Test 26 Playing with words

We can make new words by **changing** some letters.

LIGHT

fight   sight   **br**ight   **fr**ight   **sl**ight

Make some new words.

1. Change the **f** in **f**arm to **ch**.   —————————

2. Change the **d** in **d**ead to **thr**.   —————————

3. Change the **w** in **w**ay to **del**.   —————————

4. Change the **f** in **f**eed to **gr**.   —————————

5. Change the **n** in **n**erve to **sw**.   —————————

6. Change the **n** in **n**ew to **scr**.   —————————

7. Change the **d** in **d**irt to **squ**.   —————————

8. Change the **m** in **m**oan to **gr**.   —————————

9. Change the **v** in **v**oice to **ch**.   —————————

10. Change the **w** in **w**ood to **bl**.   —————————

11. Change the **l** in **l**oud to **pr**.   —————————

12. Change the **m** in **m**ow to **borr**.   —————————

13. Change the **c** in **c**urb to **dist**.   —————————

14. Change the **d** in **d**are to **bew**.   —————————

15. Change the **n** in **n**ear to **app**.   —————————

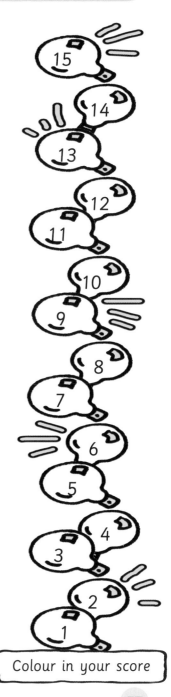

Colour in your score

Test 27 Possessive pronouns

Possessive pronouns tell us who the **owner** of something is.

These toys are not **yours**. They are **mine**.

Some common possessive pronouns are:

> mine   yours   his   hers
> its   ours   theirs

Underline the possessive pronoun in each sentence.

1.   This book is mine.

2.   This bag is blue – yours is red.

3.   The boy was sure the pen was his.

4.   Sam pointed to Anna and said, "This ruler is hers."

5.   Rex belonged to the children – the dog was theirs.

6.   "You can't have the ball. It's ours!" Tom and Ben shouted.

7.   "The model Ali broke was ours!" Amy and Emma complained.

8.   The girl picked up the purse – it was hers.

9.   Mr Smith drove a sports car but it was not his.

10.   I asked the lady if the pen was hers.

11.   Go and look at the bikes. Mine is the silver one.

12.   The children said, "These toys are ours!"

13.   "I think these smelly socks are yours!" Mum said to John.

14.   As soon as Ben won the race, he knew the prize was his!

15.   This bag has your name in it so it must be yours.

Colour in your score

Test 28 Apostrophes

Sometimes we **shorten** words and leave letters out. These words are called **contractions**. We use an **apostrophe** to show where letters are missing.

I've got an ice cream.

I've = I have

Put in the missing apostrophes in the correct places in these contractions.

1. I m

2. h e s

3. I v e

4. w e d

5. I l l

6. w o u l d n t

7. w e r e

8. h e r e s

9. d o e s n t

10. i t s

11. w a s n t

12. w h o s

13. w o n t

14. d o n t

15. y o u r e

Colour in your score

Test 29 More speech marks

When we write down what people say we use **speech marks**, or 'inverted commas'.
The **words the person says** go **inside** the speech marks.

Do you like my pet spider?

Emma said, "Do you like my pet spider?"

Put in the missing speech marks in these sentences.

1. Hello, Ben said.

2. It's nice to see you, Sam replied.

3. What a lovely day! exclaimed Ben.

4. Yes, it's so warm, Sam answered.

5. The weather forecast said it would rain, Ben said.

6. I don't think it will, Sam replied.

7. I can see a few black clouds, Ben commented.

8. I think they will pass over, Sam said.

9. Where are you off to? Ben asked.

10. I'm going to town to do some shopping, Sam answered.

11. May I come? Ben asked.

12. Yes, of course. Shall we walk or wait for a bus? Sam said.

13. Let's walk, Ben suggested.

14. I think I can feel a few spots of rain, Sam said.

15. Let's get the bus, then, said Ben.

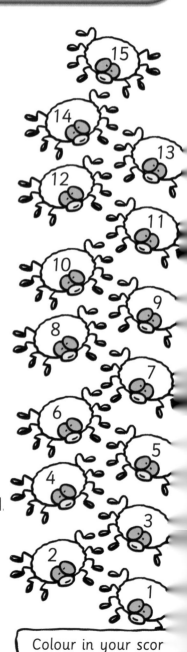

Colour in your scor

Test 30 Evaluating and editing your work

When you have written your story it is important to read things through to make sure everything makes sense. You can also use this time to add WOW words such as **shrieked** or **gasped**. WOW words can really help bring your story to life.

After you have evaluated your work, carry out a copy edit. This means you check the grammar, spelling and punctuation.

Go through the sentences and check that the spelling, punctuation and grammar are correct. Use a red pen to make your corrections.

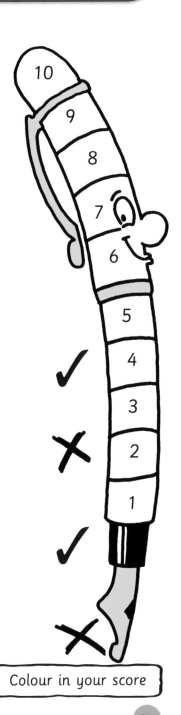

1. the ghost shimmered at the window. "A ghost!" shrieked Nora.

2. What do you mean, a ghost? Serena questioned.

3. "A see-through, wafting about, scary faced ghost!" shouted Nora

4. i think you are trying to trick me and its not even Halloween sighed Serena.

5. "I'm not. Look" nora shouted as she pointed up the stairs with a shaking hand.

6. Serena put her hands on her hips and said "Oh, OK ... I'll play along."

7. She turned and looked behind her and screamed.

8. The ghost wiggled its fingers at her and shouted boo

9. "Its real!" she squealed and ran down the stairs to follow Nora.

0. "See, i told you i wasn't making it up." Laughed nora.

Colour in your score

61

ANSWERS

Page 2

1. ight light, fright, bright
oa boat, goat, loan
ame name, frame, tame
ay play, hay, lay

2. Any words that follow the patterns given e.g. for a: main, pain, rain, vain etc

Page 3

1. a hoping
b baking
c clapping
d spinning
e winning
f losing
g shutting
h fitting
i making
j swimming
k slipping

2. a riding
b planning
c sitting
d shopping
e staring
f jogging
g slipping
h hating
i rubbing
j hitting
k raising
l shaking

Page 4

1. Sensible questions about a favourite hobby.

2. An account of what their friend said, which should read well and make sense.

Page 5

1. a unable
b unseen
c disqualify
d unusual
e disobey
f unpopular
g undo
h disappear
i disown
j untidy

2. un unwell, unkind, unlucky
dis disallow, disagree, dishonest
re recycle, return, rebuild
pre prepare, predict, previous,

Page 6

1. a huge, large
b tiny, small
c excellent, brilliant
d freezing, chilly
e unkind, mean
f after, later
g glum, unhappy
h pleased, joyful

2. Any sensible synonym for the words given

Page 7

1. a "My best friend is Max," said Joel.
b "I love football," said Rita.
c "We are going swimming today," said Mum.
d Martin said, "That is my bag."

e "I have a new puppy," said Alfie.
f The teacher said, "It is raining today."
g Dad shouted, "Do not forget your coat!"
h "Let us watch TV," said Sophie.

2. a "I am going skating tomorrow," said Heather.
b Sarah said, "That is not fair!"
c Harry sighed, "I love chocolate cake!"
d "I would like a drink please," said Lucy.
e "Look at my new bike," said Katy.
f The bus driver called out, "This is your stop!"
g "Time to tidy up," shouted Mrs Moors.
h Gran said, "See you soon!"

Page 8

1. a shines
b fly
c reads
d paints
e watches
f waits
g munches
h turn
i shuts
j rings

2. run dash, sprint, jog
make build, create, assemble
sleep slumber, snooze, doze
look see, peer, watch

Page 9

1. a walked
b went
c was
d fixed
e baked
f swapped
g drove
h hid
i worried
j tried

2. a gave
b tap
c skip
d mixed
e brought
f catch
g copy
h washed
i spoke
j build
k was
l grow

Page 10

1. a The title and author of a book.
b An explanation of why your child likes the book.
c The name of a character and the reason for choosing them as favourite.
d An explanation of the best thing that happens in the story.
e Reasoned description of the end of the story and any story resolution.

2. Make sure your child can plan a report of an event successfully.
a Name of an event.
b Reason for holding the event.

c Description of what happened at the event.
d Description of feelings after the event.
e Opinion given on taking part in a similar event in the future, with reasons given.

Page 11

1. a "Stop it!" shouted (Jack).
b "Where is my book?" asked (Sophie)
c "It is on your bed," answered (Mum)
d "Shall we go out?" suggested (Tim)
e "Good idea!" replied (Ella.)
f (Jake) grumbled, "My head hurts."
g (Lucy) asked, "What time is it?"
h (Dad) explained, "The toy is broken."
i (Sally) demanded, "Why can't I?"
j (Mum) replied, "Because it is late."

2. a said
b asked
c replied
d asked
e answered
f explained
g commented
h argued
i shouted
j insisted

Page 12

1. a a
b an
c a
d an
e a
f an
g a
h a

2. a an
b a
c an
d A
e an
f an
g an

Page 13

1. a quicker
b longest
c nicer
d late
e hottest
f fatter
g angry

2. a funnier
b closest
c biggest
d sunnier
e happier

Page 14

1. Check your child has placed a mark before Secondly, Finally and As a result.

2. Any sentences which make sense, using the connectives provided.

Page 15
1. Can your child spell the words from memory? Any sentences which contain the words given and make sense.

2. Can your child spell the words from memory? Any sentences which contain the words given and make sense.

Page 16
1. Can your child spell the words from memory?

2. Any sentences which contain the words given, and make sense.

Page 17
1. Can your child spell the words from memory?

2. Any sentences which contain the words given, and make sense.

Page 18
1. a gladly
   b suddenly
   c slowly
   d quickly
   e beautifully
   f softly
   g loudly
   h sharply
   i quietly

2. a thankful
   b perfect
   c slow
   d sudden
   e angry
   f beautiful
   g graceful
   h quick
   i certain

Page 19
1. 1 Abigail
   2 Aiden
   3 Alice
   4 Amy
   5 Anthony
   6 Arthur
   7 Ashley
   8 Attia

2. a 55
   b 18
   c 33
   d 63
   e 29
   f 12
   g 50
   h 46
   i 82
   j 6

Page 20
1. Can your child spell the words from memory?

2. Any sentences which mean the same as:
   a A person who makes a living playing music.
   b A person who rewires houses and other electrical installations.
   c A person who earns a living putting on magic shows.
   d A person who decides how the country, or a local area, is run and organised.
   e A person who works out mathematical problems, or teaches others to do so.
   f A doctor.
   g A person who tests eyes and keeps them healthy.
   h A person who carries out technical tasks, such as setting up a lab in a school.

Page 21
1. a I, my
   b you
   c I, his
   d them
   e We
   f my
   g mine
   h I, her
   i his
   j their

2. a her
   b They
   c She
   d We
   e his
   f They

Page 22
1. a sheep
   b bees
   c stairs
   d cards
   e flowers
   f puppies
   g lions
   h geese
   i monkeys
   j fish

2. a horses — herd
   b birds — flock
   c cars — fleet
   d books — library
   e musicians — group
   f dolphins — pod

Page 23
1. a Joe, my brother, is eight years old.
   b For lunch, we had sausages, chips, peas and carrots.
   c I'm wearing trousers, a shirt, socks and shoes.
   d Actually, it is quite warm today.
   e The bag split, so the shopping went everywhere.
   f In stories, the knight always kills the dragon.
   g You need sugar, flour, eggs and butter to bake a cake.
   h Anyway, it was all fine in the end.

2. a Mrs Smith, my teacher, marked my work.
   b My best friends are Chris, Sam and Jo.
   c In the end, I chose the blue coat.
   d Although it was late, we played one more game.
   e Last night, after Dad came home, we watched TV.
   f Alex, my best friend, lives next door.
   g At the zoo, we saw elephants, lions, camels and giraffes.
   h Eventually, I found the missing book.

Page 24
1. a except
   b affect
   c bawl
   d bury
   e brake
   f fare
   g grate

2. Any sentences which contain the words given, and show your child understands the meaning of the word.

Page 25
1. a 6
   b 2
   c 5
   d 4
   e 1
   f 3

2. a Find a small flower pot.
   b Fill the pot with soil, leaving a gap at the top.
   c Use your finger or a pencil to make a hole about 3 cm deep.
   d Drop a sunflower seed into the hole.
   e Cover with soil.
   f Keep soil just damp until seedling appears.

Page 26
1. a information
   b adoration
   c preparation
   d admiration
   e condensation
   f stagnation

2. Any sentences which contain the words given, and show your child understands the meaning of the word.

Page 27
1. a eight
   b vein
   c freight
   d rein
   e they
   f obey
   g sovereign
   h weight
   i prey
   j grey

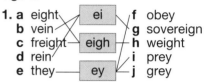

2. a I weighed out a kilogram of apples.
   b My dog obeys all my commands.
   c I did a survey about which biscuits people like best.
   d Father Christmas rides on a sleigh.
   e That horse neighed at me!
   f My neighbour is called Susan.
   g They love swimming in the sea.
   h Spiders have eight hairy legs.
   i I can see rich veins of chocolate running through this ice cream – delicious!

Page 28
1. a Understanding something
   b Dividing something into smaller pieces
   c Something to watch programmes on
   d Talking about something
   e Finding something difficult to understand
   f Entrance fee; admitting something
   g A look on someone's face
   h Being able to see

2. a invasion
   b pension
   c mission
   d session
   e version
   f expression
   g tension
   h occasion
   i passion
   j permission

Then any six words chosen, written into sensible sentences.

Page 29
1. a they run
   b they swim
   c we laugh
   d they sleep
   e they build
   f we walk
   g we eat
   h they push
   i they wish
   j we hope

2. a They pick the flowers.
   b They kick the balls.
   c We sharpen the pencils.
   d They wash the cars.

ANSWERS

Page 30

1. **a** when **d** but **g** when
   b so **e** because **h** or
   c but **f** while

2. **a** I got a drink, because I was thirsty.
   b Chris wants a skateboard, but Mum said no.
   c Luke was three when I was born.
   d We waited while Dad packed up the car.
   e I could go bowling or I could go swimming.

Page 31

1. First person accounts: b, c, f, h
   Third person accounts: a, d, e, g

2. I live in a small house in Bridge Street. I have a dog and a cat. I play netball and I am learning to play the violin. My best friend is called Leah.

Page 32

The missing prefix is in **bold**.

1. **un**pack
2. **un**well
3. **dis**place
4. **dis**trust
5. **un**fair
6. **un**happy
7. **dis**agree
8. **dis**may
9. **un**load
10. **un**bolt
11. **dis**honest
12. **un**do
13. **dis**arm
14. **dis**charge
15. **dis**please

Page 33

1. disappeared
2. spoke
3. chased
4. brushed
5. painted
6. knocking
7. drinking
8. groaned
9. pushing
10. shining
11. roared
12. crashed
13. flapped
14. hopped
15. came

Page 34

The correct phoneme is in **bold**.

1. m**oo**n
2. tr**ea**t
3. gr**ow**
4. gl**ue**
5. r**oa**d
6. cl**aw**
7. p**ai**nt
8. b**ur**n
9. **ow**l
10. th**ir**sty
11. yesterd**ay**
12. narr**ow**
13. r**ou**nd
14. s**au**cer
15. b**oi**l

Page 35

1. purple
2. a puff of smoke
3. a flame
4. strong and scaly
5. black
6. three green eggs
7. a chirping sound
8. three
9. stroked them with her paws and sang them to sleep
10. happy, pleased

Page 36

1. Where do you come from?
2. What a funny name!
3. The spaceship landed.
4. A door opened slowly.
5. Run for your life!
6. Who is there?
7. What do you want?
8. It's not fair!
9. This is terrible!
10. The sun set in the sky.
11. The bees buzzed near the flowers.
12. How did the car crash?
13. When did the letter come?
14. Stop that at once!
15. We have sausages and chips for tea.

Page 37

1. Little Bo Peep said, "I've lost my sheep."
2. The mouse said, "I ran up the clock."
3. Humpty Dumpty said, "I fell off the wall."
4. Incy Wincy Spider said, "I climbed up the water spout."
5. Little Jack Horner said, "I sat in the corner."
6. "I marched up the hill," said the grand old Duke of York.
7. "I went to London," said Dick Whittington.
8. "I met a wolf," said Little Red Riding Hood.
9. "I climbed a beanstalk," said Jack.
10. "I ran away," said the gingerbread man.
11. Hansel said, "I got lost in a wood."
12. "I went to the ball," Cinderella said.
13. Old King Cole said, "I'm a merry old soul."
14. "I made some tarts," said the Queen of Hearts.
15. "I'm very ugly," the troll said.

Page 38

1. bat cat dog
2. elephant fox goat
3. hen jaguar kangaroo
4. lion monkey ostrich
5. penguin rat seal
6. panda swan zebra
7. beetle donkey hamster mouse
8. donkey giraffe ox worm
9. cat cow crab
10. bear bird bull
11. parrot pelican pike
12. sardine shark snake
13. tiger toad trout turtle
14. gerbil giraffe gnu goat
15. badger bee bird buffalo

Page 39

1. walked
2. hopped
3. carried
4. moved
5. arrived
6. begged
7. copied
8. held
9. brought
10. saw
11. spoke
12. took
13. taught
14. wrote
15. came

Page 40

1. a mother and her child
2. a doctor, astronaut or vet
3. The mother saw that lots of people needed help when she was working as a volunteer at a shelter for homeless people.
4. yes, she loves her job.
5. work hard

Page 41

1. card, tape, paints, glitter glue, elastic
2. draw the design on card
3. cut out eye and mouth holes
4. leave the mask to dry
5. markers and glitter glue

Page 42

1. curious/anxious/surprised, wondering what the noise was
2. scared/frightened/anxious/curious
3. perhaps because she was scared
4. it was protecting the girl
5. probably looking for food

Page 43

1. chairs
2. foxes
3. coaches
4. bushes
5. glasses
6. berries
7. children
8. men
9. bike
10. box
11. bunch
12. dish
13. copy
14. lorry
15. sheep